ORAKL

ALSO BY DANIELE PANTANO

TRANSLATIONS

Fairy Tales: Selected Dramolettes by Robert Walser (2015)
Oppressive Light: Selected Poems by Robert Walser (2012)
The Possible Is Monstrous: Selected Poems by Friedrich Dürrenmatt (2010)
In an Abandoned Room: Selected Poems by Georg Trakl (2008)

POEMS

Waldeinsamkeit: Liverpool Poems (Chapter 6) (2016)
Dogs in Untended Fields: Selected Poems by Daniele Pantano (2015)
Mass Graves: City of Now (2012)
Mass Graves (XIX–XXII) (2011)
The Oldest Hands in the World (2010)
Panta Rhei (2000)
Camera Obscura (1999)
Blue Opium (1997)
Geschlüpfte Kreaturen (1997)
Blumendürre: Visionen einer Reise (1996)

ORAKL

DANIELE PANTANO

Black
Lawrence
Press

Black
Lawrence
Press

www.blacklawrence.com

Executive Editor: Diane Goettel
Book and Cover Design: Amy Freels

Published 2017 by Black Lawrence Press.
Printed in the United States.

For my children Fiona and Giacomo

CONTENTS

AUTHOR'S NOTE

I have translated. I have alphabetized. I have nothing to regret.

—Daniele Pantano
St. Moritz, Switzerland
May 2016

INTRODUCTION

Daniele Pantano's *ORAKL* melds the best aspects of conceptual poetry and traditional lyric verse. It has been said that conceptual poetry needn't even be read to be enjoyed, since its entire pleasure is usually found in the conceit the poet has adopted; once you've grasped the concept behind the poetry, you've depleted its reserves of interest and excitement. This is demonstrably untrue in *ORAKL*. It is conceptual poetry of the highest order, yet there are literary joys to be found beyond the concept.

But before I get to those, we should look at the conceptual element here. Pantano, a renowned poet and translator, has brought both of these talents to bear on his project. His process was to loosely translate all of the poems of Georg Trakl, then order the lines in alphabetical order by their first words. One further aspect of the organization is that while these lines share this overt linguistic kinship—due to the alphabetical ordering, but also due to the frequent repetition of a starting word—the lines do not share any apparent meaning relations. Like the Persian ghazal, where each couplet is meant to stand alone, seemingly disconnected from the others, yet also force by way of lyric disjoint a powerful effect on the reader, Pantano's conceptual poetry forces us to leap from line to line, navigating the voids along the way. There is a jarring-yet-also-pleasurable effect created by this structure and organization. Also, the reader will immediately notice that the title of the book is only one letter off from Trakl's name, transforming it into an oracle of sorts. This is entirely fitting, given that the lines in Pantano's collection echo the enigmatic pronouncements of an oracle from ancient myth and given that Pantano himself serves as a sort of oracular medium in translating/altering/arranging these lines.

Here is a particularly successful series of lines that illustrates in miniature what Pantano is up to in the book as a whole:

> Black skies of metal
> Black snow trickles through her arms
> Black soars the mournful ceremony of churches
> Black walls crumble on the square
> Blazing beats
> Blessed too, the flowering wombs of poor maids
>   who stand there dreaming by the ancient well
> Blind lament in the wind, lunar moonlike winter days
> Blood and weapon-fray of times past soughs in the pine ground
> Blood blossoming on the altar stone (31)

Notice the suggestive subterranean connections between the lines. We have black skies, then we have snow, and then soaring—all images that have to do vaguely with the sky yet do not form a narrative or a direct sensical connection. And later we have flowering wombs and then blood blossoming—two flower images and an association of blood with wombs and childbirth. And this loose associative quality of the progression of lines makes what otherwise might become wholly unanchored fragments a virtuoso display of free association—or not precisely free, since order is imposed as well. What we get in the end is a kind of controlled mutation, whereby each line grows into the next, though often in unexpected ways.

Aside from the overall playfulness of the concept itself, we also find here and there an attractive and sideways sense of humor, which serves to prevent the collection from veering into the realm of the overly serious, as conceptual poetry or "experimental" poetry often does. One bit of playfulness is that the letters X and Z are included, but there are no lines in those sections, merely blank pages, which I read as both a pun in one instance (the content has been X'ed out) and a playful admission that unlike the other letters, X and Z present particular challenges, given the paucity of English-language words that begin with them. But that playfulness and humor are set beside an irreverent darkness: "Angels with feces-spotted wings emerge from gray rooms" (27). We also find sincere and highly poetic lines: "Exalted is the silence of the forest, greened darkness / and the mossy creature fluttering up when night falls" (41). In short, *ORAKL* navigates several poetic techniques and tonal registers with enviable dexterity.

Renowned novelist, poet, and translator David R. Slavitt has said that to translate is to collaborate with the original author, and I can think of few examples where this is truer than in *ORAKL*. It is as though, through some oracular feat, Trakl has been channeled through and by Pantano in order to collaboratively produce this fine collection.

Pantano writes, furthering the classical theme which permeates this utterly contemporary work that:

> From branches in wild shivers silver the night wind's
> lyre of Orpheus sounds forth in the dark mere fading
> away by greening walls (44)

And indeed, Pantano plays the role of Orpheus with aplomb, channeling Trakl as both muse and oracle. These poems bridge several poetic traditions and bring several layers of aesthetic and intellectual pleasure. We would do well to read and reread them and carry them long with us.

—Okla Elliott
May 2016

"A voice comes to one in the dark."
—Samuel Beckett

"Language is worth as little as life itself, for it is life itself."
—Elfride Jelinek

ORAKL

A

A bare tree is writhing in black agony
A bearded face full of pity turned away quietly
A beast breaks shyly through the yellowed reed
A beast steps silently from tree arcades
A bell rings and the shepherd leads his herd of black
    and red horses into the village
A black angel emerges from it
A black silence already trembles
A black storm threatens above the hill
A blackbird trills piteously
A blackbird's startled call
A blackish swarm of flies
A blessed sound falls from apple branches
A blossoming outpour leaks away very gently
A blue beast wants to bow before death
A blue breeze got caught brightly
    in the ancient elder tree
A blue cloud has sunk onto me in the dusk
A blue deer
A blue deer quietly bleeds in the thicket of thorns
A blue face softly leaves you
A blue moment is only more soul
A blue moth crawled from its silvery cocoon
A blue smile on his face and strangely pupated
    into his quieter childhood
A blue water grieves
A blue's glance breaks from crumbling cliffs
A bony horror strikes when black the dew
    drips from bare willows
A boy lays his brow in her hand

A boy sets a fire near the hamlet
A bread smell and pungent spice
A breath of fever circles a hamlet
A breath of warm manure drifts by
A bright corpse bending over a dark thing
    and a dead lamb lay at my feet
A bright day of childhood glides after you
A bright number stands on a stone
A brother of yours dies in an enchanted land
A brown tree stands secluded
A burning rider explodes from the hillside
A burning wheel, the round day
    of earth's endless agony
A bush rocks yellowhammers in its lap
A calm modesty enters cool chambers
A carillon sounds into the small brown garden
A child stands in silhouette soft and tender
A child walks on the parched meadow
A child with brown hair
A child's skeleton shatters silver against the bare wall
A cloth of hair laid on a bier
A cold luster darts across streets
A crimson cloud shrouded his head, which fell mutely
    over his own blood and likeness, a lunar face
A crimson mouth arches in the hazel leaves
A cross looms boldly amid sparkling stars
A cross towers among wild vines
A dead face follows the boy
A dead man visits you
A delicate corpse lay silent in the dark chamber
A deranged seer, he sang a song
    by crumbling walls, and God's
    wind devoured his voice

A dog has died in front of her chamber
A dog lunges along the paths
A dog runs past a dreaming man
A dream
A dreaming soldier sings his mournful song
A drunken faun is dancing in golden mists
A dry-boned fool leads the lepers' dance
A dying beast greets in parting
A face has sunk drunkenly into the grass
A faint glockenspiel sounds in Elis's breast
A fantastically mad sequence
A farmhand intones the prayer
A faun with dead eyes stares
A firelight blazes in the room
A firelight flashes from the cottages
A fisherman pulled with a net of hair
    the moon from a freezing pond
A flight of nuns
    blows by on the landing
A fluttering flowerbed paints
    symbols, rare embroideries
A fountain falls in the darkness
    of chestnut branches
A fountain lilts
A gentle monk folds the lifeless hands
A gentle silence lives in bread and wine
A glowing boy
A golden barge
A golden cloud follows the lonely
    one, the grandchild's black shadow
A golden day glows to its end
A golden ray breaks through the roof and flows
    onto the siblings, dreamlike and confused

A golden tumbrel wheels through the clouds
A good shepherd leads his flock along the forest edge
A graveyard shudder
A gray stench permeates the air
A greenish dusky mountain stream
A guitar hums
A halo falls upon the girl who waits
A harsh wind sneers in my ear
A hay-rick flees through gray, yellowed
    and skewed
A heart freezes in snowy silence
A herd loses itself in the red forest
A horse's skull stares from the rotten gate
A host of wild birds migrating
    to those lands, beautiful, different
A house glimmers to pieces, strange and vague
A jangling of coins
A light rouses shadows in the rooms
A light shaft freezes in the clouds
A line of birds greets on its journey
A line of birds slips into the distance
A little bird trills like crazy
A little fish flashes past and fades
A lonely fate glides down the forest edge
A long afternoon
A long time the moon gazes in
A lover stirs in black rooms
A lute's mocking strums
A magnetic chill hovers around this proud head
A masculine red bending over mute waters
A melancholy birch
A minute of mute destruction
A minute of shimmering silence

A monk, a pregnant woman there in the crowd
A mournful smile about her mouth
A nest of scarlet snakes rises languidly
　　in her ruffled womb
A nightly wreath of violets, wheat
　　and crimson grapes is the year
　　of the one who watches
A noble fate ponders down
　　the valley of Kidron
A pale angel
A petrified head storms the sky
A procession of wild horses
A pure blue flows from its decayed shroud
A purple flame went out by my mouth
A quake of church chimes upswells
A quartet's final chords
A rabble of flies whirls around the flowers
A rabid dog is walking through a barren field
A red dress flies through a crowd of children
A red flame leapt from your palm
　　and a moth burned in it
A red shadow with a blazing sword
　　burst into the house, fled with snowy brow
A red ship on the canal
A red that shakes you like a dream
A red wolf strangled by an angel
A rolling drum, black foreheads of warriors
A roof of parched straw, the black earth
A room wants to brighten palely for the murderer
A rose-horrid lightning bolt flashes
　　into ringing spruce trees
A rotting lineage lives
A saint emerges from his black stigmatic wounds

A scent of bread escapes from a shop
A scent of milk in hazel branches
A scent of thyme hovers in the gold
A sex
A shadow, he walked down the bridle path
    beneath autumnal stars
A shepherd decays on an ancient stone
A shepherd mutely follows the sun
    that rolls from the autumn hill
A shrub full of larvae
A shy beast emerges from the edge of the forest
A silence dwells in black treetops
A silence dwells in empty windows
A silken triad fades to a single note
A silver hand
A sinister corsair
A small bird sings in the tamarind tree
A small fish glides swiftly down the brook
A sober clarity shows itself in the grove
A soft violin sounds from the courtyard
A song accompanies the guitar that rings out
    in a strange tavern
A square darkens grim and sinister
A stooping scribe smiles as if mad
A strange life dwells in the wine
A stranger by the evening hill, who weeping lifts
    his eyelids above the city of stone
A strip of meadow soughs windswept and faint
A sultry mist brews on the waters
A sweet playmate, a rosy angel approached him, so that
    he, a gentle animal, slumbered into the night
A tattered flag steaming with blood, so that a man
    eavesdrops in wild melancholy
A thorn bush sounds

A thrush frolics with them
A tree, a dog steps back behind itself
A tree burned down in red flames
A vile procession full of filth and mange
A village that dies away piously in brown images
A waxen face flows through alders
A whispering that drowns in troubled sleep
A white angel visits the three Marys
A white shirt of stars burns the carrying shoulders
    and God's vultures mangle your metallic heart
A white steamer on the canal carries bloody plagues upstream
A white stranger enters the building
A wild beast standing still in the peace of the ancient elder tree
A wild pain grows in the farmwife's womb
A wind whines morosely across the meadow
A wolf mauled the firstborn to pieces, and the sisters fled
    through dark gardens to reach the bony old men
A yellow head turned away, the child, silent
Ablaze the bushes waver
Above falling cities of steel
Above Mount Calvary God's golden eyes open in silence
Above parks in grief and pale
Above the black patch
Above the broken bones of men
Above the forgotten paths of the dead
Above the sea
Above the sleep of cows
Above the vanished path
Above the white nymphean mirror
Across the pond
After midnight, drunk on crimson wine
    you leave the dark district of man, the red
    flame of his hearth
After shadows gliding into the dark

After the one striding, the stranger
Again and again you return, melancholy
Again night returns and a mortal thing laments
Again the delicate corpse meets
Again the forehead darkens in moonlit stone
Against the gray sky lines of wild birds follow
Alas, one evening by the window, when
    a gruesome carcass, death, emerged
    from crimson flowers
All about the forests are wondrously mute
All at once glittering rain rushes down upon the roofs
All guilt and red agony
All roads lead to black decay
All this is unspeakable, O God, we
    fall to our knees, shaken
Allow one last glance up
Along autumnal walls, he, a young
    sexton, quietly followed
    the silent priest
Along summer's yellow walls
Along the hill, by the springtime pond
Already in the black throng of horses and carts
Already night beckons for a journey to the stars
Already the pondering man's forehead is dawning
Already the rosy overgrowth begins to clear
Already the swallow prepares for its journey
Also an age-old white head bends over
Always
Always chill's dark figure follows the wayfarer
Always the blue bells of evening sounded
    from twilight towers
Always the night bird shrieks in bare branches
    over moonlit striding

Always the sister's lunar voice
Always the white night leans against the hill
Always you walk down the green river
Amid an airless beech tree silence
An ancient lullaby fills you with dread
An angel's blue poppy-eyes open
An animal face stiffens with blue, its holiness
An echo of dancing and violins
An empty coffin loses itself in the dark
An even higher future that resembles you
    as you resemble yourself
An evening sinks through the arched window
    mild and soft
An evil heart laughs out loud in beautiful rooms
An icy wind sounds at the village walls
An old man spins sadly in the wind
An old square, chestnuts black and wasted
An open window, at which a sweet hope stayed behind
An organ chorale filled him with God's tremors
An organ comes playing in
An organ sighs and hell laughs
An unspeakable face emerged from the chalky wall
    —a dying youth—the beauty of a lineage returning home
Ancestors' marble changed to gray
Ancient legends
And a blackish cloud shrouded
    my head, the crystal tears of damned angels
And a blue wellspring rushed in the ground
And a canal suddenly spews fat and blood
And a cock crows beneath the door
And a dark voice spoke from within me
And a dreadful stench from the privy stinks after them
    through which the ghostly moonlight shudders

And a faraway friend writes a letter to you
And a little lamp of goodness shines in his heart
And a pulsating swarm of gnats
And a sinister guest gently closes the door
And a suggestive tree rustles above his deranged head
And a swarm of flies buzzes
And a white beast collapses
And Afra's smile red in a yellow frame
    of sunflowers, fear, and gray humidity
And all around hills and forests sparkled
And all night the female dancer's steps ring
    through the greenery
And an abundance of leaves is falling
    onto the stone path
And an ancient water sings
And an angel in the grove
And angels step silently from the blue
And another suffers
And are the lonely one's companions
And as I lay there gazing and dying, fear
    and my deepest pain died within me
And as though dead she glances over
And at night they plunge from red shudders
    of the star wind, like frantic maenads
And at times something deceased steps
    from decrepit blueness
And back to the field
And barely feel the hour hands move
And beautifully painted by sunshine
And bees still gather with earnest diligence
And before Satan's curses
And beneath elm trees, you walk
    in familiar conversation down
    the green river

And blacker and blacker melancholy veils
    the departed head, gruesome lightning frightens
    the nocturnal soul, and your hands tear open
    my breathless chest
And blood pounds in their temples
And blue lakes, above them the sun
And bows down low over mournful waters
And bread and wine are sweetened by hard work
And bursts the pines into flames
And called in night and desolation
And carried a small rosy child in his black coat
And coaxed by abasement
And crimson blood flowed from the wound
    beneath his heart
And crouched together she freezes
And crowd house and stores that are filled
    with grain and fruit
And dark readings of the flight of birds
And devoted to your will, ever moved
And dissolved figures also flee in smoke
And earth's pilgrimage a dream
And eyelids dazed by fear flutter softly
And falls overcome to the ground
And festive the air in spacious courtyards
And flutter upon black-crossed paths
And following old custom an evening bell sings
And following the sister's shadow
And follows ferns and old stones
And from blackish gates emerge angels with cold brows
And fruit drops from the trees
And fruit ripens peacefully in a sunlit pantry
And gently the dead friend's hand moves
And girls who embrace the Lord's body like poison
And glass and chest in twilight

And glimmers silver from tangled leaves
And God's heaven falters black and sheds its leaves
And he saw the starry face of purity
And her mouth is like a wound
And her womb awaits the heavenly bridegroom
And here and there a cross on a barren hill
And his murderer searched for him
And his tears fall hot and clear
And horridly an empty garment decays
And hunters descend from the forest
And I crossed the dormant pond
    on a curved skiff, and sweet
    peace brushed my stony brow
And in holy blue luminous steps ring forth
And in rose wreath and rows
And in the garden the friend's silver face remained
And in the twilight rock niches
And it was noon and the animal's silence was immense
And it was the murmur of the forest
And later her shadow gropes along
    cold walls, surrounded by fairy tales
    and holy legends
And leaves drift, trumpets blare
And leprosy has turned their foreheads bald and raw
And lifts its hands to God's golden shrine
And lovingly smoothes forehead and robe
And my soul's echo—the wind! that sneers and sneers
And naked bones dance past
And night devoured the cursed descendants
And now and then buds crackle gaily
And often smile in anguish
And often the golden and true show themselves
    to gentle madness

And opens the soul fearful and wide
And our wide eyes follow the passage of birds
And paints panic's grim specters
And plays with her eyes black and smooth
And pure his face
And quietly the hand of the dead woman
    seizes his mouth
And raised its cold eyelids over him
And rats scream in the yard
And ravens splash in bloody gutters
And rolling constellations in the black briar
And scurry this way, that way, like flutes
And shadows enclose it, like hedgerows
And she breathes hard upon the pillow
And she is like a shadow
And she lies utterly white in the dark
And she sees her filthy bed
And she shudders before its purity
And she slips past the gate
And she staggers into the forge
And she stares shaken with pain
And shimmering a drop of blood fell
    into the lonely one's wine
And silver bloom the flowers of winter
And sink in darkness, dreaming
And slowly lowers its heavy eyelids
And slowly the gray moon climbs
And slowly the strangers depart once again
And snow and leprosy drop from his forehead
And softly
And softly an ancient stone touches you
And softly blood poured from the sister's silver
    wound, and a rain of fire fell upon me

And softly open to strange constellations
And something gold
And something unborn sighing from blind eyes
And something you mistake for a fire
And sometimes lustful glances meet
And sometimes rose-colored mosques
And sometimes you can hear them fret over carrion
    they smell is somewhere
And sometimes you float, light and wonderful
And sometimes you see them in fretful rest
And space becomes a grave
And sparrows flutter over bush and fence
And spew blood in winding thorns stiff and gray
And strangely scattered in the evening wind
And suddenly they point their flight northward
And sunflowers sink over the fence
And terror seizes the heart
And the animal's scorching wilderness
And the autumn gold of the elm tree
And the awakening at the edge of the twilight forest
And the bell in the valley drones mightily
And the blue bright sky
And the blue hyacinth had just bloomed at the window
    and the old prayer appeared on the breathing one's
    crimson lip, crystal tears sank from his eyelids, crying
    for this bitter world
And the boy's radiant blue shadow rose
    in the dark, a gentle song
And the boy's rosy angel appeared softly before him
And the chill of an evening spring
And the cock crows to the last
And the cool blue embraces him mightily and the burning
    remains of autumn

And the cypresses breathe calmly
And the dark
And the day dissolves in the green
And the delight of green
And the flowers of summer that ring lovely in the wind
And the flying veils of night pass away in bursts of flames
And the footsteps grow quietly green in the forest
And the gentle flutes of autumn
And the gloomy voice laments
And the head of the waif stiffens with the agony
    of a golden day
And the heart rings softly in the night
And the heavenly distances open in bright purity
And the house is well in order
And the lonely bird's squall above the green silence of the pond
And the lonely one's brow quietly greens again
And the melodious sound of its spiritual years
And the moon chased a red animal from its cave
And the moon eavesdrops from the trees
And the moon that glowing sinks into sad waters
And the mother's lamenting shape staggers
    through the lonely forest of this mute grief
And the murderer's shadow in the twilight corridor
And the oars silently row as one
And the peace of the meal
And the red deer, the green flower
    and the babbling spring
And the redness creeps slowly through the torrent
And the scythe clashes in the field
And the shadows of the damned descend
    to the sighing waters
And the silence of the elder
And the silver voices of stars

And the sky leaden and vast
And the stranger's steps ring through the silver night
And the sun sets beyond the hill
And the sweet chanting of the resurrected
And the twelve assembled
And the white figures of the light
And the white voice spoke to me
And the wilderness by the shore greens
    darker, delight in rosy wind
And the wilderness of her eyebrows
And the women's dark lament died sighing
And the yard lies long deserted
And the yellow flowers of autumn bend mutely
    over the pond's blue face
And their breath flows sweeter through the night
And their immeasurable melancholy overflows
    into the evening blue
And then climb down to earth, you glorious one
And then pales to nothing in the mirror
And there the mother rots with her child
And these hopeless laments for the dead
And they pour the wine and break the bread
And they shriek eagerly as if mad
And things unborn rest in their own peace
And thinks the mother's somber face
And those dead step from bare rooms
And to the mild lamp inside
And toads slept through the young leek
And tranquil eyes look all around in their purple caves
And trickle away like a funeral cortège
And walks, a pale angel, through the empty grove
And wanders slowly on the flood
And wake your much-loved slumbering woman

And we cried in our sleep
And weakened by her protests
And when I bent over silent waters
    with silver fingers, I saw my face
    had abandoned me
And when I drank of it, it tasted more bitter than poppy
And whirl in through the open window
And with helpless gestures
And with shrills the scythes swing ghostly
    back and forth in time
And yet, and yet
And you move your arms more beautifully in this blue
And you see lights that have lost their way
And your brother looks at you softly
    with nightly eyes, that he may rest
    from thorny travels
And your eyes are staring at you like steel
And your forehead rages through the soft green
Angels with feces-spotted wings emerge from gray rooms
Appearing, the one sleeping descended the black forest
Are so quiet
Are soundless in the reeds
Are the clouds, white, wisping
Around dark rims of weathered fountains
Around the pale flowers on a stifling flood
As his head sinks into the black pillow
As if man's golden likeness were devoured
    by the icy wave of eternity
As if the shadows of those long dead hovered above it
As in a dream she's met by laughter
As though a brazen gate were slamming shut
As though a tender corpse followed in the shadows
As when blue water roars in the rocks

At evening a whispering rises on the islands
At evening drift bloody linens
At evening on the terrace we got drunk on bronze wine
At evening: steps come through black land
At evening the autumnal forests resound
At evening the cuckoo's lament falls silent in the forest
At evening the place lies desolate and brown
At evening when we walk down dark paths
At midnight
At night a shepherd leads his flock across the meadow
At night a snowy wellspring above mossy steps
At night above the barren meadow
At night drink the icy sweat that runs from Elis's crystal brow
At night he remained alone with his star
At night his mouth broke open like a red fruit, and the stars
    began to sparkle above his ineffable grief
At night I found myself on a heath
At night stars seek, Good Friday's child
At night the sleeper found them beneath the pillars in the hall
At night they scream in sleep under olive limbs
At nightfall they carried the stranger into the chamber of the dead
At nightfall you hear the bats shriek
At red breasts and in black lyes
At the awakening the bells rang in the village
At the cool feet of the penitent woman
At the forest edge
At the forest edge, lighting the sinister paths
At the gate by dark paths
At the pond of Triton
At the sight of the ruined graveyard on the hill
At the stream the women still wash
At the window whose stare is barred
At this hour I was the white son in my father's death

At times he recalled his childhood filled
   with sickness, horror, and darkness, furtive
   play in the garden of stars, or how he fed
   the rats in the twilit courtyard
At vespers the stranger looses himself
   in November's black ruin
At your feet
At your mouth
Autumn: black pacing along the forest edge
Autumn in rooms
Autumn is quiet, the spirit of the forest
Autumnal graveyard, holding his mother's frigid hand
Autumnal reeds rustle their laments
Autumnal retinue
Autumn's golden breath
Autumn's path and crosses enter evening
Autumn's sinking
Avanti!

B

Back to her, this word for her
Bare tree in autumn and silence
Bare trees by the hill
Bare trees sough in the evening garden
Bare walls grow dark
Barren field and an acre's soil
Bathed mildly by the scarlet luster of stars
Bats flutter about in the cloister
Bats flutter up with dark faces
Beating sheaves of yellowed wheat
Beautiful: O sadness and crimson laughter
Become silent and hug each other like fools
Before glazed eyes blue images juggle
Before I wandered in night and desolation
Before the decayed ancestral marble
Before the glass door, soft and white
Before the image of eternal grace
Before the Savior's agony on the cross
Before the silence of winter follows
Before the singing breath of the lonely one
Begone! Begone!
Behind cross and brown hill
Behind the hill winter has come
Beneath an arch of thorns
Beneath ancient oaks
Beneath arches made of stone
Beneath bare oak trees he strangled a wild cat
    with icy hands
Beneath damp evening branches
Beneath dark fir trees
Beneath mutilated willows, where brown children play

Beneath oak trees
Beneath oak trees we rock in a silver boat
Beneath old cypress trees the tears of nightly images
    gather by the well
Beneath rotten branches, past walls filled with leprosy
Beneath sinister firs
Beneath sucking trees something dark
    walks into evening and doom
Beneath the eaves a cooing fades
Beneath the golden branches of night and stars
Beneath the hazel bush, the green huntsman
    is gutting an animal
Beneath the round sky
Beneath the stars
Beneath withered trees, he drunkenly breathed
    in the scarlet of those sacred robes
Beyond the hamlet
Bitter snow and moon
Black dew drips upon your temples
Black frost
Black is the sleep
Black mignonettes in the dark
Black one, die in the rock
Black skies of metal
Black snow trickles through her arms
Black soars the mournful ceremony of churches
Black walls crumble on the square
Blazing beats
Blessed too, the flowering wombs of poor maids
    who stand there dreaming by the ancient well
Blind lament in the wind, lunar moonlike winter days
Blood and weapon-fray of times past soughs
    in the pine ground
Blood blossoming on the altar stone

Blood flows from lunar feet, blooming on nocturnal paths
    where the rat darts screaming
Blood-spattered linens billow
Blooming apple-branches sway in moist air
Blossoms in the flood's reflection
Blowing down at the threshold
Blue asters bow and shiver in the wind
Blue doves
Blue drone of organs
Blue flower
Blue shadows
Blue soul, dark wandering soon severed us
    from loved ones, others
Bluely the night's plumage whorls
Blueness, the mothers' lament for the dead
Bones climb from the family vault rotten and gray
Bones of graves rise from the carpet
Border and blackness of the forest, twilight fears in the green
Branches bared by the föhn wind beat against the window
Breaking in the snow of the abyss
Breath of the unmoved
Breathe God's blissful peace
Breathless he entered the decaying house
Bright instruments sing
Brightness in the theater
Bring asters from dark fences
Brown chestnuts
Brown girls' rough songs scattered
    in falling leaves
Brown pearls trickle through dead fingers
Buckets plunge up and down
But a bloody ground seems very mournful and grim

But a muter mankind bleeds softly in a dark cave, forging
    the redeeming head from hard metals
But always the black flight of birds moves
But always the self is black and near
But gruesomely the sparse green withered by the windows
    of the nocturnal ones, and the bleeding hearts
    still contemplate evil
But he descended the stone steps of the Mönchsberg and died
But he lifted a stone and threw it at him so he fled
    wailing, and sighing the angel's soft face
    faded away in the shadow of the tree
But he sang softly in the green shade of the elder tree
    when he awoke from an evil dream
But he spent his days in a dark cave, lied and stole
    and hid, a blazing wolf, from his mother's white face
But he stood before her suffering mutely and buried in his steely hair
But he was a small bird on bare branches
But how all this growing seems so sick
But in the evening the shadow of the deceased quietly entered
    the circle of his grieving family, and his crystal steps sounded
    across the greening meadow by the woods
But like bones the steps sway over snakes asleep by the forest
    edge, and the ear always follows the frantic shriek of the vulture
But on the pasture spilled blood, red clouds in which a raging god
    lives, gathers softly, lunar chill
But quietly you came in the night while I lay awake
    on the hill, or raging in a spring storm
But shining, lovers raise their silver eyelids
But shrub and beast followed him
But spring drips in shivers
But the soul takes comfort with a righteous gaze
But there was no one there to lay a hand on his forehead

But this grief has no agony
But through the stone wall you see
    the starry sky, the Milky Way, Saturn, red
But when a dark melody haunts the soul
But when he walked with fervid thoughts beneath bare trees
    along the autumnal river, there appeared to him a blazing
    demon in a coat of hair, his sister
But when I descended the cliff path, madness seized me
    and I screamed loudly in the night
But with soft steps you walk into the night
By a bare wall
By autumn walls
By crumbling walls
By the bare gates of the slaughterhouse stood
    a crowd of poor women
By the brook that runs through the yellow fallow field
By the edge of the bluish fountain
By the evening pond
By the fence the poppy wilts white
By the fence where sunflowers grow
By the graveyard the blackbird jests with the dead cousin
By the hill the evening wind ends softly
By the mill boys light a fire
By the path a woman piously suckles her child
By the river the tavern still sounds mild and low
By the rubbish a chorus of rats' spoony whistles
By the suet-light in the cellar pit
By the windows the swoosh of a circle dance
Bygone evening that now sinks across the mossy steps, November

C

Calm was our step, round eyes in the brown chill of autumn
Calmly childhood dwelled in a blue cave
Candlelight in rooms
Castle and hill glow in the distance
Chased by bats, he plunged off into the dark
Cheats the hungry one of recovery
Chestnuts waste away in the heavy golden glow
Child, your sickly smile followed me softly in sleep
Childhood, softly footsteps fade away by the black hedge
Childhood's patience and silence
Children gladly listen to fairy tales through the long evening
Churches, bridges, and hospitals stand ghastly in the twilight
Clawed blossoms loom in the trees
Climbed down the soul
Clingclang! A sickle reaps
Clingclang! In the fog hear it echo
Closer the blue wellspring soughs the women's plaint
Clouds over silent forests that are draped in black linens
Clouds reveal themselves at evening
Clouds, shot through by light, the Last Supper
Coarse ferns, firs
Cold and pale the damp brow bends over the filth
    where the rat roots
Cold metal steps on my forehead
Come, love, to the tired workingman
Comes again through the evening gray
Convalescents warm themselves by the windows of the hospital
Cool our burning brows with shivers
Cooler colors of violet blossom
Coolness and autumn in lonely rooms

Corn bleeds in the shade of old roofs
Crazed and drunk on wine
Crimson dew of night and all around the stars are going out
Crimson plague, hunger that bursts green eyes
Crimson the fruit ripened on the tree, and the gardener
    shook his calloused hands
Cringing at his laughter
Crippled birches moan in the wind
Crippled trees stare by the black wall
Crisscross in red storms blow
Cross and evening
Crossings over dark waters
Crowns shine in the churches
Crows flutter up around a vile meal
Crows that scatter, three
Cruel bells ring through black branches
Crumbling gods stood in the garden, mourning in the evening
Crystal angels chime once more
Crystal childhood gazes from blue eyes
Crystal flowers
Crystal voice, in which God's icy breath dwells
Curse you, dark poisons
Cursed fare
Cut are wheat and grapes
Cyclopean rocks preserve the chill of dark years

D

Daedalus's spirit hovers in blue shadows
Daily the yellow sun comes over the hill
Damnation, when the dreamer's heart overflows
    with evening's crimson afterglow
Dancers rise from a black wall
Dark autumn arrives full of fruit and plenty
Dark breath in green branches
Dark dew is bleeding down
Dark love of a savage race, whose day rushes
    away on golden wheels
Dark silence of childhood
Dark trumpet blare passed through
    the elm tree's wet golden leaves
Dark voices died in strife
Darkened by the slumber of leaves, the dark gold
    of withered sunflowers
Darkens the lithic chamber
Darker the waters engulf the pretty play of fish
Darkness that descends upon the gorges
Darting across strange stairs, he met a Jewish girl
    and reached for her black hair and took her mouth
Dead Rachel wanders through the farmland
Dead, we rest beneath the elder bushes
Death is bitter, the fare of the guilt-ridden
Death's pale flowers shiver on graves mourning in darkness
Death's pure images peer from church windows
Decay glides through the rotten chamber
Decay that softly darkens the leaves
Decay trickles through the walls
Decayed lips suck

Decayed, love and autumnal reverie
Decayed shacks, decrepit emotions
Decayed things float in the slop, the föhn wind coos softly
    in the small brown garden
Decay's black wings flutter up
Decay's embers glow in the depth
Deep in slumber the frightened soul sighs
Deep is the slumber in dark poisons, filled with stars
    and the mother's white face, the stony one
Deep the wind in broken trees
Defoliated stars
Delicious the young wine and nuts
Delicious: to stagger drunk in the darkening forest
Deserted forests resound in all directions
Deserted mountains
Despair, night in brains of grief
Dew dripping slowly from a blooming thorn
Dew drips on the face
Didn't she stand with pleading hands?
Distorted things, grimacing flowers, laughter, monsters
Do you recall, you fool, you buffoon?
Downstairs an angel with crystal fingers is knocking on the gate
Drawing water at dusk
Dreaming a stablehand sings in the dark
Dreamlike a sound in the brown village
Dreamlike the candle's glow weaves
    paints this young flesh decayed
Dreamlike the torrent's dark spirits rattle the heart
Drowned in the soft lyre-play of his madness
Drunk on dark frosts, the larva
    bends over the huntsman's sleep
Drunk on dark poisons, the silver larva
    bent over the shepherds' slumber

Drunk on the dark song of poppy juice
Drunk with a bluish scent
Drunk with air, eyelids soon sink inward
Drunk with the juice of poppies, the lament of the thrush
Dusk is falling
Dust spins in the reek of gutters
Dying away beneath greening trees
Dying away beneath the olive tree
Dying out of nightly eyes, falling stars
Dying sounds of metal

E

Each returned from her tarnished pilgrimages
Each year the head bows more deeply
Earlier lives glide by on silvery soles
Earnest was his life in the shade of the tree
Echo in putrid darkness
Echo in threatening thunder
Elai! your face bends over blue waters speechless
Elderberries, flutes soft and intoxicated
Elders blow over softly along the path
Elis, when the blackbird calls in the black wood
Enchanting clouds of roses
Encircled by clouds of golden tobacco
Endless agony, that you caught God
Endymion emerges from the dark of ancient oaks
Enough, when drunk with wine the head sinks into the gutter
Enraptured this mad sequence scattered on yellowed paper
Equally dark the day of year, woeful childhood
Erected by stone upon stone on the plain
Evening and the somber scents of green
Evening changes sense and image
Evening cloud
Evening continues to sound in damp blue
Evening föhn wind in March
Evening in a deserted tavern
Evening returns to the old garden
Evening sounds in deep bells
Evening strikes such a deep wound
Evening, when the blackbird sang near the twilight wall
Evening wind softly soughs at the window

Evening's blue dove did not deliver reconciliation
Everything that pleases her becomes divine
Evil
Eyes of lovers who suffer more gently
Exalted is the silence of the forest, greened darkness
    and the mossy creature fluttering up when night falls

F

Fading of a gong's brown-golden echoes
Faith, hope
Falling stars
Familiar steps on the darkening stairs, the sight of
    browned rafters
Fantastic shadows plunge off the roof ends
Far away a cock cries
Far from leaved cottages, sleeping shepherds
Far from the turmoil of time
Farmhands and maids have begun their meal
Father's silence, when sleeping he descended
    the twilight spiral stair
Fear, death's dream grievance
Fear, you poisonous snake
Female monk! cloister me in your darkness
Feverish, he sat on gelid steps, raging against God that he would die
Fields of asters, brown and blue where children play by crypts
Figures: men and women, the deceased walk in cool
    chambers to prepare their beds
Figures walk stiff as wax through embers and smoke
Filled with beautiful chariots, bold riders
Filled with reverie and peace and wine
Filled with snakes, moths, spiders, bats
Fire purifies the torn night
Fire sparks in the forge
Flames, curses
Flames flicker in the beds
Flare up, your stars in my arched eyebrows; and the heart
    rings softly in the night

Fleeting is the gold of days
Fleeting shapes go down
Flickering shivers on the beautiful pond
Flies buzz around her mouth
Flies buzz in yellow palls
Flitting, wavering at the open window
Föhn winds color the sparse shrubs brighter
Followed by dark years
Followed by eternal night
Followed humbly
Following again the blue lament of evening
Footsteps through a fog of blood
For always a blue deer, something keeping watch
    beneath twilight trees, follows these darker paths
    moved by nightly melodious sound
For bread and wine are blessed by the hands of God
For he softly raises his eyelids over something human
    which is far away
For the patient one wakes ever more radiantly
    by petrified steps from black minutes of madness
For the white child
Forehead that spies in itself in fear
Formless objects of ridicule flit, cower
Forsake, when your brow gently bleeds
Foulness rises from the earth
Fragrance of mignonettes; a fiery sense of evil
Fragrant apples on the dresser
Frantic circle dance
Freely the brook is greening where his foot takes silver steps
Friend, the leaved footpaths to the village
From a dark corridor the golden figure
    of the girlchild emerged

From branches in wild shivers silver the night wind's
    lyre of Orpheus sounds forth in the dark mere fading
    away by greening walls
From brown walls emerges a village, a field
From hands asters sink blue and red
From the brown bright churches peer
    death's untainted tableaus
From the graveyard, a golden chill wafts
From the slaughterhouse down into the calm river
From time to time a scant word drops
Frost and smoke
Frost, smoke, a footstep in the empty grove
Fuming above stony wasteland

G

Games of lust
Garden of strange adventures
Gentle bells tremble through the breast
Gentle is the blackbird's lament
Gentle madness
Gentle sonata, gay laughter
Gentle spirit, sighing in falling waters
    in surging pine trees
Gently the sun sounds in rosy clouds above the hillside
Ghostlike the föhn swells the wandering boy's white nightgown
Girls are coming in as well
Girls stand in archways
Gladly the soul listens to the white magician's fairy tales
Gleaming avenues loom from the clouds
Gleaming with stars
Glimpse into opal: a village wreathed by seared vines
God has bent your lids
God, into your gentle hands man lays the dark end
God spoke a gentle flame to his heart
God, take pity on these women's hellish agony
God's blue breath drifts into the garden hall
God's breath gently wakes string music in the haze
God's forehead dreams colors, feels the gentle wings of madness
God's lonely wind sounds against black walls
God's silence I drank from the grove's well
God's wrath furiously lashes the forehead of the one possessed
Gold drips from the bushes dull and flat
Golden blooms the tree of mercies from the earth's cool sap
Golden cloud and time
Golden clouds

Golden evening silence
Golden eye of inception, dark patience of the end
Golden-eyed owls flutter around her head
Golden flare the fires of the races all around
Golden-red garments, torches, singing of psalms
Golden the sunflowers sank across the garden fence
    when summer came
Goldfish glisten deeply on the water surface
Good and evil are prepared
Grandmother lights golden candles
Grape leaves scatter whirling into blue
Grapes ripen to gold on the slopes
Grazing evening clouds in the peace of seared plane trees
Great dying and the singing flame of the heart
Great is the guilt of the one born
Great is the silence of the fir forest, the grave shadows by the river
Green branches bend willingly over something dreaming
Greetings, desolate graveyard
Groping over summer's green steps
Guitars strum, red coats shimmer
Gulls shriek by the window frames

H

Hammer and anvil clang without pause
Hands of nymphs cause death's grave darkness
Hands stir the vintage of blue waters
Hanging linens sail
Hatred burned up his heart, lust, when in the greening summer
    garden he attacked the mute child, recognizing his own
    deranged face in her radiant one
He begged for a piece of bread by the gates of the monastery
He fell like a stone into nothingness, for in the shattered mirror
    a dying youth, his sister appeared
He returns and walks the green shore
He silently walked up Mount Calvary
He truly loved the sun climbing crimson down the hill
Hear the villagers rejoicing
Heart, bend more lovingly now over the calm sleeping woman
Heavy shadows spread over brown manure
Heavily the stormy fir trees sank over them, and the red huntsman
    emerged from the forest
Her cheeks turn waxen and pale
Her dirt-stiffened hair filled with black tears
Her eyes graze round and golden in the dusk
Her face floats through the village
Her hair catches in the bare branches
Her image peers at her in the mirror
    strange, silver in the twilight-glow
Her yellow hair flutters
Here a capable life shows itself in silence
Here boys play
Here man is cheerful and mild
Here the shadow of Eve, the hunt, and red coins

His breath drinks icy gold
His cheeks near flames that flicker in the window
His dead brother stands behind him, or he descends
	the old spiral staircase
His dreams filled the ancient house of his forefathers
His hands are steaming with blood, and the animal's shadow
	sighs in the leaves above the man's eyes, brown and silent
His madness, and white brows and his demise
His mouth's dark lament
His ruined face gray in the moon
His star appeared above him in gray night
Holy night
Horror often seizes them in the raging roar of wheat
Horsemen along fields of rye, empty mills
Horses dive from the fountain
Hospitals filled with crazed fever-screams and curses
Hostile things followed him through gloomy alleyways, and his ear
	was shredded by iron clatter
Hour of grief, the sun's mute gazing
House and twilight garden of white people
Houses loom from mute threats
How beautifully image follows image
How pale the mothers are
How sad this evening
How was it once
Human ruins decay in the gloom of the old asylum
Humble shacks, paths scattered in chaos
Humility bleeds so softly
Hunger-mad crows at dusk
Hunger's crimson curses
Huntsman's call and blood-baying

I

I am a shadow far from sinister villages
I broke my black steed's neck in the nightly woods, when madness
    leaped from his crimson eyes
I dream after their brighter fates
I follow the miraculous flights of birds that in long flocks, like lines
    of pious pilgrims, vanish in clear autumnal skies
I want to be a horseman
I will always be with you
I wish to walk along the forest's edge, a mute thing
    from whose speechless hands the sun of hair sank
Icy winds moan in the dark
If a blue deer were to think of its path
If he might only forget his fate and the thorny spike
If only the cool head would finally shatter
Ignite the trepid sky with a blazing torch
Images of clouds, flowers, and people
Immense is the silence of the ruined garden
In a boat down the blue river
In a deserted passageway, his own bleeding figure
    appeared to him stiff with filth
In a dilapidated shack
In a garden the notes of a gentle game are sounding
In a great cloud of golden light
In a meadow children are playing ball
In a solitary chamber you often invite the dead one
In a stony wall
In autumn leaves turn crimson
In blue shivers the night wind came from the hill, the mother's dark
    lament dying again, and I saw the black hell in my heart
In cool and useless rooms instruments rot

In dark rooms, the mother's face turned to stone, and the boy
   was burdened by the curse of his degenerate lineage
In gardens bells sink long and low
In his grave the white magician plays with his snakes
In old cellars the wine mellows into the golden clear
In old stone the toad peers from crystal eyes
In pain it shall still offer friendly guidance
In pure hands the peasant carries bread and wine
In red leaves full of guitars
In rigid darkness their longing arms delicately entwine
In somber conversations man and woman
   recognized one another
In sweet and stale rot
In the beeches jackdaws flutter
In the black hour of evening
In the brightly-winged breeze
In the brown woodwork
In the childlike gardens
In the city of stone
In the clear blue
In the courtyard, bewitched by milky twilight glow
In the courtyard, he, a wild animal, drank from the fountain's
   blue waters until he shivered with cold
In the dark of brown chestnuts the young novice's figure fades
In the darkening garden, the step and silence of the dead boy
In the darkness of the chestnuts a blue floats
In the darkness of the chestnuts a red laughs
In the deep silence of noon
In the distance the sinking sun grazes on a crystal meadow
   and its devastatingly wild song, the bird's solitary call
   dying in blue calm
In the elderberry before her cell
In the evening

In the evening again over my head
In the evening an icy wind blows from our stars
In the evening garden, where pious disciples walked long ago
    warriors now, waking from wounds and star-dreams
In the evening he enjoyed walking across the ruined
    graveyard, or he gazed at the corpses in their twilit chamber
    of death
In the evening he found a stony wasteland, a dead man's escort
    into the dark house of the father
In the evening he walked past the mountain with a cripple
In the evening seeds and the golden shadows of melancholy
In the evening summer
In the evening the father became an old man
In the evening the fisherman raised the heavy nets
In the evening the plague hems her blue gown
In the evening the resurrected meet on rocky paths
In the evening the white water sinks in funeral urns
In the evening through the old garden
In the evening vale, the blue wellspring's crystal billow rushes
In the evening, when the bells ring peace
In the evening's breezes, wafted past in clear breezes
In the fever bed, stared at by a brash moon
In the forge pounds a hammer
In the garden apples fall dull and soft
In the garden, dissolved in brown lyes
In the garden the sister speaks kindly with specters
In the gardens disorder and movement
In the gold there a scent of thyme
In the gray, filled with illusion and ringing bells
In the hazel bush
In the holy peace of the vineyard's distant dying light
In the house
In the lonely hours of reverie

In the low, smoke-blackened hall
In the next room the sister plays a sonata by Schubert
In the old park our steps resound softly beneath tall trees
In the old tavern off-tune violins are screaming more madly
In the park siblings behold each other trembling
In the rosemary: a breath of graveyard odors fades away
In the salty sea of misery
In the shadow of ancient arches the drunkard broods
    upon the migration of wild birds
In the shadow of the tree
In the shadow of the walnut tree, the ancient elder
In the shadowy regions of shattered pine trees
In the shadowy vault of the walnut tree
In the silence
In the silence the fearful soul's lonely lyre-play dies
In the silence of the moor
In the stove a hideous glow of embers
In the tavern on rotten wallpaper
In the thicket of thorns a deer softly dies
In the twilit vale
In the valley the ancient bells and gloomy hamlets rest peacefully
In the wheat stern scarecrows whirl
In the window's darkness
In their beauty's shimmering abundance, letting the dead
    dream more deeply
In this hour the eyes of the witness fill with the gold of his stars
In this night on warm pillows yellowed by incense
In thorny wilderness, the dark one followed the yellowed paths
    through the wheat, the skylark's song, and the soft silence
    of the green branches, that he might find peace
Incense streams from rosy pillows
Ineffable is the flight of birds, encounter with the dying
Inside huddle of fear's ghosts are

Into air that shivers of rapture
Into every basket fell putrid meat and guts
Into green voids filled with rot
Into his cottage falls a tepid beam
Into the black and empty sockets of her eyes
Into the city made of stone
Into this dream-locked garden
Into water startled by a wild rebellion
It is a brown tree that stands alone
It is a hissing wind that circles empty shacks
It is a light that dies in my mouth
It is a light that the wind has extinguished
It is a room they have whitewashed with milk
It is a stubble field on which a black rain falls
It is a tavern a drunkard leaves in the afternoon
It is a vineyard, burnt and black holes full of spiders
It is an empty boat that drifts down the black canal in the evening
It is an island in the South Seas there to receive the sun god
It is fine to walk in the sun
It is the tender time of love
It rolls through her long hair
It seems you can also hear terrible screaming
It sounded like love
It tarries patiently beneath dark arches
It wants to see stars and angels
It was night; a snowy wellspring above mossy steps
Its blue fruit have fallen away
Its broad silence lives in the forest

J

Jackdaws circle above the pond
Jagged lightning lights the brow
Joy sheens not very far away
Joy, when in cool rooms an evening sonata resounded

K

Kill yourself!
Kindly she transforms darkness into light, the distant
   into the near

L

Last year's withered reed still rustles
Laughter flutters up, blows away
Laughter in a crimson bower
Laughter still glows, golden chime of a bell's final strokes
Laurels grace the noble one's white temples
Leaves drop red from the ancient tree
Lepers are reflected in black waters
Lepers, rotting perhaps that night, read confused omens
    from the flight of birds
Let the song also remember the boy
Let us pray
Lies and sodomy burned his head in twilit rooms
Life is hard, and the peasant swings his steel scythe
Lifeless the sea grows dark
Life's daydreams in shacks near the forests
Light drives out the stony night with a magnetic whip
Lightning driving blinding clouds
Lights are burning beneath the arcades
Like a carrion in the underbrush and dark
Like a woman burdened by a dire portent
Like lovers who embrace each other in sleep
Like shadows standing behind black shrubbery
Like the hammer hard and coarse
Like your belly so beautifully out
Listening in the leaves or ancient rock
Listening to the blackbird's gentle lament
Lithe maidens grope through the backstreets
    of night, that they may find the amorous shepherd
Little slender women and satyrs in unison
Lonely people are seized by a dark terror

Lonely winter's eve
Long ago, the monk wrapped in a blue coat saw her piously
    painted on church windows
Long he lay in a stony field and gazed with amazement
    at the golden tent of stars
Long peal of evening bells
Long rings the evening bell
Long the ear follows the paths of the stars in the ice
Look! already dusk is falling
Love blesses bread and wine
Love, hope, so dew drips from fiery eyelids
    into stiff grass—relentless!
Love, when in black corners the snow melted
Lovers among butterflies glow again and swing happily
    round stone and number
Lovers bloom toward their stars
Lovers raise their rosy eyelids
Lovingly too the silence of the room enfolds
    the shadows of the old
Lust, tears, stony pain, the Titans' dark legends

M

Magnificently does the year thus end with golden wine
    and fruit of gardens
Maidens walk through moist blueness and at times gaze
    from eyes filled with nocturnal bells
Man: hunter or shepherd
Man is beautiful when seen in the dark
Mankind lined up before fiery gorges
Many a traveler arrives
Marching drums, the shouting of the guard
Mary rests white and fair
Measure and law and the lunar paths of the departed
Melancholy of the fuming city
Melancholy! the eagle's lonely lament
Memory: seagulls gliding across the dark sky
    of masculine dejection
Merrily the lonely ones on silent paths walk sinless
    with God's creatures
Mighty princes' fine shields
Mignonette scent streams through brown greenery
Mixing sound and golden light, sound and light
Moistening it, a pink drop of dew hangs
Monks, pale priests of lust, their madness adorns itself
    with lilies dark and lovely
Monstrous is the silence inside stone
Moon, as if a thing deceased emerged
    from a blue cave
Moon-bright sonata
Moon cloud

Moon-white the chill of stone enfolded the waking
   brow, the striding of the shadows on crumbling
   steps, a rosy circle dance in the little garden
More clearly in the silence of red beeches
More deeply he loved the sublime works of stone; the tower
   that nightly storms the blue sky of stars with hellish grimaces
More justly the blooming hedge delights him, the young seed
   of the peasant and the singing bird, God's gentle creature
More often from black gloom the owl screeches after the drunken one
More often in crimson gloom the owl screeches after the drunken one
More piously you know the meaning of dark years
   to his star
More radiantly the white stranger raised his hands
Morning shivers hard and gray
Mother appears in pain and dread
Mother carried the child under the white moon
Mother must fear for her small child
Motionless the reeds loom by the bluish pond, the thrush
   falls silent at night
Mountains: blackness, silence, and snow
Mournful guitars are flowing
Mouth and lie broke crimson in the cool
   of a decaying chamber
Music hums in the grove of afternoon
Mute Saturn guides a wretched fate
Mutely pleading for poor souls
My face died in a hell of stone
My soul's echo, the harsh wind

N

Narcissus in the final chord of flutes
Night and speechless a forgotten life
Night and terror of sunken forests
Night appears in silence, a bleeding deer that slowly
    sinks down by the hillside
Night appears, the angel of rest, on the threshold
Night flutters up on drunken wings
Night waves to dying soldiers
Nightly he lived in a crystal cave and leprosy grew
    silver on his forehead
Nightly shadows
Nightly the rush of blue water through the bedrock
Night's apparitions: toads emerge from silver waters
Nights filled with tears, fiery angels
No echo carried it
No longer played, a glockenspiel goes down at night
No one is in the house
Nobody loved him
November evening
Now and then clouds swim above the hill
Nuns hurry like silk in a dream

O

O bitter death
O blue luster she wakens in the panes, framed
    by thorns, black and stiffly rapt
O dark fear of death, when gold
    died in a gray cloud
O darkness; the sweat that pearls on the icy brow
    and the sad dreams in wine, under the smoke-blackened
    beams in the village inn
O despair that falls to its knees with silent cries
O fool! O buffoon!
O gentle drunkenness on the gliding boat
    and the blackbird's dark calls
O gentleness of the lonely soul
O gold's horrific laughter
O green flower–O silence
O heart gleaming across into snowy chill
O how dark is this night
O how everything sinks into darkness
O how full of fear and lowliness they seem
O how gruesome the walk by thorny paths
    when everything's aware of its guilt
O how just, Elis, are all your days
O how lonely ends the evening wind
O how long, Elis, have you been deceased
O how mild is autumn
O how old is our family
O how sad is this reunion
O how severe is the hyacinthine face of twilight
O how silent a walking down the blue river, pondering
    the forgotten, when in the green branches the thrush
    called something strange to its doom

O how silent was the house when the father went forth into darkness
O how softly the cross rose in the dark soul
O how softly the dark face faded into black fever
O how softly the garden withered in autumn's brown silence
O how softly the light burned
O how somber is the face of the cherished dead
O how their hair is stiff with shit and worms, that in which
    he stands with silver feet
O how they disturb the brown stillness, in which a field
    sends itself into ecstasy
O human
O if only it were spring outside, and a lovely bird
    were singing in the blossoming tree
O image in the toad-pool sweet and clear
O lonely standing before waters still and white
O mankind's decayed shape: forged from cold metals
O mournful shadows on the walls
O mouth! that quakes through the white willow
O my brother we climb blind clock hands toward midnight
O my silver arms still sound with wild thunderstorms
O our lost paradise
O pain, you blazing vision of the great soul
O poverty, beggar's soup, bread, and sweet leek
O prouder sorrow! you brazen altars, today an immense pain
    feeds the spirit's hot flame
O restless the twilight head listens or the hesitant steps
    follow the blue cloud on the hill, and the grave
    heavenly bodies too
O silence of yellow and red flowers
O sweet Helios
O sweetness that satisfies the sparrow's hunger
O the animal's mossy glances
O the army's glowering melancholy; a radiant helmet sank
    clashing from a crimson brow

O the birches in the storm, the dark beast
   that shuns its deranged paths
O the birth of man
O the bitter hours of ruin
O the black angel who emerged from the tree's core
O the blood that flows from the resounding throat
O the boy's form shaped by crystal tears
O the crimson sweetness of the stars
O the cursed descendants
O the damned
O the darkness
O the decayed, how they silenced hell with silver tongues
O the diligence of bees and the green leaves
   of the walnut tree, the passing storms
O the evening that enters the dark villages of childhood
O the expired disk of the sun
O the fiery tear wept into the night
O the flute of light; O the flute of death
O the forest that softly lowers its brown eyes, when
   from the lonely one's bony hands the purple of his days
   of ecstasy fades away
O the glowing angels scattered by the crimson evening wind
O the gray face of terror, when he opened his round eyes
   over a dove's cut throat
O the greening cross
O the hell of sleep; dark alleyway, small brown garden
O the hour, when with a mouth of stone he sank away in the garden
   of stars, and the murderer's shadow came over him
O the house cricket's ancient call
O the hours of wild ecstasy, the evenings by the green river, the hunts
O the lust of death
O the madness of the big city
O the moist shadows of the mead, the pacing animal
O the nearness of death

O the nightly ones
O the night's gentle bundle of cyan
O the red hours of evening
O the signs made of hair in bright sunlight
O the silver fish and fruit that fell from stunted trees
O the soul that softly hummed the song of the yellowed reed; fiery
    piety
O the soul's nightly stroke of the wing
O the stony hill
O the sunken chime of evening bells
O the twilit spring paths of the pensive one
O then he opens his slow hands, rotting in crimson sleep
O then he opens his slow hands, to receive
    the light, sighing in vast darkness
O then it slowly opens its cold hands
O then you too shall bow your head
O there the golden footbridge
O to dwell in the soulful blue of night
O you brazen times buried there in the sunset
O you broken eyes in black mouths, while the grandson
    peacefully mad ponders the darker end alone
O you children of a dark lineage
O you crusades and burning torments of the flesh, the fall
    of crimson fruit
O you dark eyes that keep staring at me
    as you glide by
O you hunts and castles, evening calm
O you joyful one
O you nights and stars
O you psalms in fiery midnight rains
O you signs and stars
O you silent mirrors of truth
O you times of silence and golden autumns

O you towers and bells; and night's shadows fell on him like stone
O you villages and mossy steps, glowing sight
O your smile in the dark, so sad and evil a sleeping child grows pale
Odor of tar; the quiet rustle of red plane trees
Often by the well at dusk
Often her eyelids lower heavy and wicked
Old bones shimmer through crumbled walls
Old people glide silently into the stiller evening; beautiful
    leaves wither softly
Old squares keep sunlit silence
On a black cloud, you, drunk on poppy, travel the nightly pond
On a black skiff lovers crossed into death
On a blackish barge he traveled down the iridescent streams, full
    of crimson stars, and greening branches sank peacefully
    down on him
On a dark plain we meet ourselves with shepherds
    and white stars
On distant fields scythes mow
On foot through the twilight of summer, past sheaves
    of yellowed wheat
On his way home he came across an empty castle
On one side of his elephant ivory brow the lonely
    one reveals the glory of fallen angels
On the ridge a deer bleeds softly to death
On the wailing autumn wind, the cries of the unborn
On the walls the stars have died
On their return the shepherds found the sweet body
    putrid in the thorn bush
On willows catkins dangle gently in the wind
Only night around me and desolation
Only the brook flows still and calm
Or Elis's steps ring through the grove, the hyacinth
    one, fading away again beneath oaks

Or he lowers his head in crimson sleep
Or in cold night the sisters' white cheeks
Or it bends in silence over the sleep of a watchman who sank
    down in his wooden hut
Or it leans faded over the murderer's cold brow in the dark
    of the hallway; worship, crimson flame of lust; dying, the sleeper
    tumbled down the black steps into darkness
Or shepherds sing at night and stags enter
    into the circle of their fires
Or the lute sounds full of dark rapture
Or there are screams in sleep
Or weeping they open their filth-spattered robes
    to the balm scent wind blowing from the rosy hill
Or when, holding his father's calloused hand
Or when in the evenings he crosses Saint Peter's
Or when, in the evenings, holding the old man's
    bony hand, he walked to the crumbling city wall
Orphans sing sweetly at vespers
Our pale figures appear before us
Our silence is a black cave from which sometimes
    a gentle beast emerges
Over blackish cliffs the glowing whirlwind
    plunges drunken with death
Over our graves bends night's shattered forehead
Over stubble-field and path
Over the path of bones, the boy's hyacinth voice
    quietly speaks the forest's lost legend
Over the white pond the wild birds have passed away

P

Pain and hope
Pain petrifies the threshold
Pale and blind girls play in the hazel bush
Pale wave shattering on night's shore
Parched grass in abasement kneels at her feet
Past gardens, autumnal, singed with red
Past the thorny hedges
Patiently the hard life keeps silent in the shacks
Peaceful the union of the gates' blackish splendor
Peacefully the dark animal encounters a rosy man
Perfect is the silence of this golden day
Perhaps the ineffable flight of birds, the unborn's path
    past sinister hamlets, to lonely summers
Perhaps the memory of an earlier life that rises
    and falls with warm winds
Perhaps there flies are singing over a carcass
Perhaps this hour has stopped
Perhaps too a child is weeping in its mother's lap
Pierce, black thorn
Pious custom is beautiful
Play louder you violins
Poppy from a silver cloud
Prayer and amen softly darken the evening chill
Preparing an ominous future for its white grandchildren
Pure sky in the branches
Purity! Purity!
Purple murices crawl from broken shells
Purple vines climb around clay cottages
Put it out

Q

Quiet is the laughter of the joyful one, music
    and dance in shady cellars
Quietly a candelabrum burned inside, and silently I hid
    my head in crimson linen; and the earth cast out
    a childlike corpse, a lunar body that slowly stepped
    from my shadow and with shattered arms sank down
    stone ledges, flocculent snow
Quietly an organ goes
Quietly and long he gazed into the toad's star-eyes, felt the coolness
    of the ancient stone with trembling hands, and gave voice
    to the sacred legend of the blue wellspring
Quietly from black forests a blue beast
Quietly preparing itself for an act
Quietly the waters rush in the sinking afternoon
Quietly the white night draws near

R

Radiant abyss of the sun
Raging magician, under whose blazing coat
    the warrior's blue armor rattles
Red the ore sounds in the shaft
Red trickles down through the dark
Red-hot the stablehand swings his hammer
Reeds tremble yellow and tall
Remains in a room of stone
Resonant with melodious sound and soft madness
Resounding love
Resting in the hazel bush she plays with his stars
Restless wandering through wild rocks far from evening
    hamlets, flocks returning home
Ringing green and red before the window
Rocks, Elis, your heart on a lonely sky
Rocks in a small black gondola through the crumbled city
Rolling away more sinister; night enfolds the dying warriors
Rosy daffodils in the sepulchral vault of night
Rot glows in the green pool
Rotten fruit falls from the branches
Rotting human beings rise
Rows of roses

S

Sails, masts, ropes flash on the river
Sails upon the canal
Saint Thomas dips his hand into the stigmata
Satisfied we stroll along red walls
Saturdays the cottages are filled with tender singing
Saw that snow fell onto leafless branches
Say how long ago since we died?
Scarlet banners, laughter, madness, trumpets
Scarlet banners plunge through the maple's grief
Scattered villages, fen, and pond
Scent of mignonettes bathes the female
Scent of mignonettes strays through the sick window
Seagulls hover silver-gray
See how the damned scatter in mad haste
Self-spilt blood runs from the heart, and in black eyebrows
    nests an ineffable moment: dark encounter
September evening: the shepherds' dark calls echo
Shadows are spinning upon the hill
    fringed black with decay
Shadows dance on wallpaper
Shadows glide across the pillow
Shadows now in night's cool womb, mourning eagles
Shadows on yellow wallpaper; in dark mirrors the ivory
    sorrow of our hands forms an arch
Shapes leap up from water drains
She chases after the wild sparks
She narrows her inflamed eyelids
She opens her holy womb to you
She sways in feverish dreams
She works to herself in the cell

Sheds flee through little gardens
    brown and wasted
Shepherds buried the sun in the stark forest
Shepherds, we once walked along the twilight forests
Shivering the night comes in
Shocking is the decline of this generation
Shooting lights sway around scorched dung
Shuddering beneath autumnal stars
Shy, staring into a colorful life
Sickle moon in a rosy gorge far from praising shepherds
Sickle moon—with the soft embrace of lovers
Sighing, a boy's shadow rose in me and gazed at me
    from radiant crystal eyes, so I sank weeping
    beneath the trees, the vast vault of stars
Sighing, the fallen angel beholds his image
Signs and stars sink softly into the evening pond
Silence dwells in blue chambers
Silence in the nightly room
Silence of villages
Silent and forgotten the cool body melts in silver snow
Silent branches ponder: the murmur of leaves
Silent his step found the town by evening
Silent I sat beneath smoke-stained beams
    in a deserted tavern, lonely drinking wine
Silent night
Silent people walk in measures
Silent stands a still birch
Silently a dark deer encounters
Silently again the moldering forest receives the babbling wellspring
Silently the myrtle blooms over the dead man's white eyelids
Silently they gathered at the table; dying, they broke
    the bleeding bread with waxen hands

Silver in tired lids flickers through
    the flowers in the windows
Silver step in the shadow of the stunted apple trees
Silver the evil flowers of blood shimmer
    on his brow, the cold moon in his broken eyes
Silver the rosy day emerged from the eastern gate
Silver waters trickle down the forest steps
Silver your hand gropes for fruit
Sing, sing, joyful world!
Singing people walk with reluctant steps
Singing pilgrims and the blood-spattered linens
Sister of stormy melancholy, see a fearful barge is sinking
Sister, when I found you by the lonely glade in the forest
Sister, your blue eyebrows softly beckon in the night
Sleep and death, the grave eagles rushing
    round this head all night
Sleeping the footbridge arches across the torrent
Sleepwalking you hear her fountain swell
Slow stairs of moss
Slowly the feverish forehead bows to the white stars
Slowly the grape ripens, the wheat
Slumbering in its hyacinth hair
Sly perfume in flowered windows whispers
    of incense, tar, and lilac
Small blue flowers float around
Small green flowers sway around her
    and her face has abandoned her
Small red fish in the pond
Smiling innocence reflects you
Snapped black fir trees in the night
    storm, the steep citadel
Snow fell, and blue darkness filled the house
Snow has fallen

Snow quietly falling from a crimson cloud
So bluish it glows toward the city
So he found the white figure of a child in the hedge
　　of thorns, bleeding for her bridegroom's coat
So he lifts the snake with his slender hand, and his heart
　　melted away in burning tears
So painfully good and true is all that lives
So sacred green the oak trees
So softly a lunar beam closes the crimson marks of melancholy
So something forever mystifying will renew
　　itself again in high beauty
So speechlessly the homeless one follows
　　the wind with his dark brow
So that a dark madness shivers from the sleeper's brow
So that he quietly raised pale eyelids over his snowy face
So the cyclopean clouds scatter, in which winter, breaking
　　loose from the earth, is still howling
　　its threats with icy shivers
So the fading stars ring out dancing
So the lonely one's figure turns inward
So the stranger trembles in the dark
So tranquil the child peers into the night, with eyes
　　that are utterly honest
Soft and melodic is a walk past cheerful rooms
Soft invalids glide through things autumn-browned
Soft singing of childhood
Softer something dying now the brother's lament
Soft sounds of birds in flight
Softly a golden summer rises in the blinded window
Softly a rotting trellis goes
Softly an open window rattles; tears well up
Softly footsteps ring in the grass
Softly from a hill a shepherd goes

Softly sounding in yellowed stone
Softly the doe's scream freezes at the forest edge
Softly the olive tree's blue silence sinks along bare walls
Softly the pond mirror blinds
Softly the stone building tolls
Softly the yellow corn rustles in the field
Softly yellowed moons spin over
    the young man's fever-linens
Softly young mothers sing
Someone gazes through the door
Someone has abandoned this black sky
Someone left you at the crossroads, and you
    gaze back for a long time
Someone whispers in the garden below
Something calm plays before a tavern
Something dark delights the scent of violets, swaying wheat
Something dark often appears striding along
    walls that stand in autumn
Something dark soothes the brook's purl, the damp shadows
Something dead mutely leaves the crumbled house
Something pale awakens in a stifling chamber
Something sick cries silvery
Sometimes a sleigh rings in the distance
Sometimes howls swell from muffled motion
Sometimes the wind carries to the window the timid
    ringing of a bell
Sonja smiles soft and fair
Sonja's life, blue silence
Sonja's step and gentle silence
Soon a village seems to bow like a ghost
Soon all around the stars grow pale
Soon fish and deer slip away

Soon stars will nest in the tired one's eyebrows
Soon violets will bloom
Soon you hear it in black defiles—that stars are
    already perhaps appearing too
Sore and naked the nun prays
Soundless their bills shear
Sounds glide wonderfully through the gray
Sounds of blue deer beneath the trees
Sounds of your narrow smile
Sounds through the spiritual night
Sparrows clamor in the fields
Sparrows plunge from balmy skies
Speechless!
Speechless I lay beneath the ancient willows, and the blue sky
    was high above me and full of stars
Spiders search my heart
Spring and summer and the righteous one's
    lovely autumn, his quiet steps past
    the dreamer's dark rooms
Spring clouds rise over the dark town that veils
    the nobler ages of monks
Spring dawns in shades of blue
Spun in deep blue and gold
Star and blackish passage vanished
    along the canal
Star and furtive sparkling
Star and night forever follow
Stiff with filth and the dust of stars
Storm-pity, the snowy peaks all around
Strains of a guitar softly accompany autumn
Strange are the nocturnal paths of man
Stranger!

Strangers listen on the steps
Stretched out frail upon the bed she wakes
    full of sweet terror
Stride down and gird the dreaming head
    with tender-bright blossoms
Stride down now, titanic fellow
Strolling again in the old park
Strolling through the dusky garden
Such anxious days are coming
Sudden scream in sleep
Suddenly the south wind rattles the gate
Sun, clouds, flowers, and people
Sun, thin like autumn and shy
Sunflower, softly bent over Sonja's white life
Sunflowers glow along the fence
Surrounded by pale moons
Swallows draw insane signs
Sweet fragrance of apples
Sweet smell of incense and pears
Sweet torture consumed his flesh

T

That was long ago
That you caught God
The air is burning!
The ancestors' utensils lay decayed
The apple trees sink bare and calm into the colors
    of their fruit spoiled black
The arbors shine brightly, since young women
    walked past here in early morning
The arch of your brow
The arms release a thing deceased
    hemmed in by the sadness of a carpet
The autumn moon lives quietly at your mouth
The barberry bushes have vanished, all year they dream
    in the leaden air beneath the pine trees; fear, green
    darkness, the gurgle of one drowning
The bare tree furiously knocks on the stone wall
The beggar there by the old stone seems deceased in prayer
The bell's long rings in November's night
The birches there, the black briers
The bird voice of the deathlike man
The birds tell you faraway tales, into which cloister bells peal
The black lambs by the abyss
The black swords of falsehood
The blackbird laments in the leafless branches
The blackbird's lament falls silent
The blind maid appears in the courtyard
The blind spread incense in festering wounds
The blond, radiant ones
The blooming wind awakens
The blue flows with mignonettes

The blue of my eyes has died in this night
The blue of springtime waves
    through snapping branches
The blue pond
The blue river runs down lovely
The blue rustling of a woman's dress turned him
    into a pillar of stone, and his mother's nightly figure
    stood in the doorway
The blue shape of man walked through his legend
The blue spring at your feet, mysterious
    your mouth's red silence
The blue swell of the glacier
The blueness sinks onto glass and chest
    that keep them in mind
The boy wakes wild from dreams
The boys' crazed dreams in the seared strands of willows
The boy's golden war cry
The boy's mouth slips away strange and wise
The boys' uncouth game pleases the friend
The bread and wine of a just life
The brother's gentle song by the evening hillside
The brow stirs the water's blue motion
The brown village
The burning brow dies down in calm and silence
The burning melancholy of a raging god
The candelabrum flickers silver
The candle shines softly in the dark room
The caretaker's children stop their play and search
    for the gold of heaven
The carpenter joins mighty beams
The carpenter squares wooden beams; the mill grinds
The cat's shadow glides blue and slender
    from the rotten roof hemmed by coming misery

The childlike fruits of the elder tree bend in wonder
    over an empty grave
The child's hands flow through her hair
The chords of his steps filled him with pride
    and contempt for mankind
The church soars up like a prayer
The church square is dark and silent
    as in the days of childhood
The church tower's shadow returns to the flower window
The city's white walls sound incessantly
The clang of horns echoes in the meadows
The clock that strikes five before the sun
The cloud lost something golden above the path
The cloud travels over the pond's mirror
The clouds wander deep and clenched in black
The clowness weeps with unbound hair
The cold grave holding man's burning heart
The cool autumn night arrives
The cool chamber which death reconciles
The cricket's ancient song dies down in a field
The crimson body shatters against gruesome reefs
The crimson torments, lament of a great lineage that now passes
    piously in the lonely grandchild
The crimson wave of battle
The cross keeps watch on every grave
The crystal wave slowly dying
    by the crumbling wall
The dark flight of jackdaws; a guard entered the square
The dark plain appears without end
The dark song of an old man fades away
The dead man with white hand paints
    a grinning silence on the wall
The dead man's face moves by the window

The dead orphans lie beside the garden wall
The dead soldier makes the call to prayer
The death chambers are wide open
The decayed, the turned-blue, opens his eyes
The decaying cliffs everywhere
The deer comes tremulous from its lairs, while a brook
    flows by in silence
The deer's crystal meadows
The delicate limbs of lovers part
The dew beads in the bushes
The drunken woman is seized by sweetest intuition
The ear hears night's sonata notes
The earth is hard; the air tastes bitter
The earthen faces crumbled down grinning
    in the trunk's brown branches
The echo of black steel
The elder bush heavy with fruit
The elders in a peace of brown shadow
The evening bell and the beautiful community of man
The evening bell chimes long
The evening too is blue
The evening's brown and blue colors
The ever cool one, when a springtime storm
    resounds by the greening hill
The faded luster of lovely summer days
The fair-haired teacher guides Angela's walk
The fall moon shines white in the yard
The fathers' immense resentment, the lament of mothers
The father's voice, like a blind man's, sounded
    and conjured up dread
The fervent lament of the deer
The field gleams white and cold
The fields shimmer without end

The fish rises reddish in the green pond
The fish stand still
The fisherman glides softly in his blue skiff
The fisherman pulls a large black fish from the pond
    of stars, face full of cruelty and madness
The flame belongs to the palest brother, his clandestine laughter
    in crimson hair; or it's a place of murder, where a stony path
    runs past
The flight of birds is full of harmonies
The flight of birds resounds with ancient myths
The flood still carries heaven's golden load
The flowers died by the evening pond
The föhn blows out of something black
The forehead stirs the dying leaves
The forest
The forest is beautiful, the dark animal
The forest paths, the singing blackbird
The forest, which spreads itself demised
The forest's edge traps blue animals
The forest's surge red and sallow
The fragrance and sadness of the ancient elder tree
The fruit shines crimson through black branches
    and in the grass a snake is shedding its skin
The garden is inside the evening
The gardener mows by the wall
The gate remained locked today
The gentle hum of bumblebees
The gentle orphan still gathers sparse corn
The gentle wheat swells softly and raptly
The ghost of evil watches from pale masks
The girlchild I long fell for
The golden cloud above the pond
The grandchild who drinks milk and stars

The grape is ripe
The graves of the dead open
The gray and stony hush, the cliffs of night
    and the ever-disturbed shadows
The gray wind, fickle and vague, flushes the dusk
    with decayed scents
The green beckons with a peaceful gesture
The green crops softly lead aside, the deer a shy chaperone
    on mossy forest paths
The green forests have gathered by quieter shacks
The green forests of our homeland
The green stains of rot on their beautiful hands
The green summer has become so quiet
The grieving reeds rustle in the pond
The grove's ancient sorrow
The hamlet in autumn and peace
The hands of man carry brown vines, while the gentle pain
    in his gaze lowers
The harsh swings of the reaper's scythe
The hawk cries hard and bright
The head nods away into the dark of the olive tree and dies
The head of the unborn sank away like silver
The head that mutely abandons its legends
The healing flood beckons the lepers
The heart grew white by the forest
The horror of death seizes the sick
The hour came when he saw shadows in the crimson sun
The hour of our dying, Azrael's shadow that darkens
    a small brown garden
The humble find their sites well prepared
The humming of bees, the flight of the crane
The hunt descends red from the forest

The immense fear of the gruesome red sunset
    in storm clouds
The lament that sounds forth like crystal in the dark
The last gold of fallen stars
The laughing blood plunges from the hill
    where the dying sun rolls
The leaves on the chestnut no longer stir
The leaves run down red
The leper's brow listens up under the bare tree
The little men, little women, sad companions
The lonely evening pond
The lonely one wanders with his heavenly bodies
The lonely one will soon slip away, perhaps a shepherd
    on dark paths
The lonely one's face, his golden stride
The lonely wander quietly in the hall of stars
The lovers' brows sank in shivers
The madman has died
The maid blows out a lamp
The maids listen, dumb and mute
The maple's black burden sinks through the window
The market is empty of summer fruit and garlands
The mask of a night bird
The memory of legends told
The men perform warlike dances
The mercy of radiant arms enfolds a breaking heart
The mignonettes there at the window
The mirror pond shatters with a bang
The monastic specter strolls through bright days
The moon always shines into decayed rooms
The moon chases terrified women
    from bleeding thresholds

The moon rises; night is turning blue
The moon wraps itself in green veils
The mother sings softly in her sleep
The mother's silence; beneath black firs sleeping
    hands open up, when crumbling
    the cold moon appears
The mouths of the blessed broke purple
The murderer simpers pale in the wine
The mysterious face of the Sphinx, on which my heart
    wishes to bleed out
The nearby grove sings children to sleep
The night is black
The night wind delves through her hair
    bathed by lunar glow
The noon hour strikes slowly
The nymphs have abandoned the golden forests
The old man's wife dances in blue slime and fogs
The old women go to the well
The one gazing, the holiness of blue flowers
The orphans' garden, the dark asylum
The others flee through darkening arcades
The pale man lives inside the blue crystal, his cheek
    leaning against his stars
The pale shape of the sister emerged from putrid blueness
    and thus did her bleeding mouth speak
The patient one humbly submits to pain
The peach glows a red in the leaves
The peasants' brown foreheads
The peasant's calm gestures rest quietly
The petrified head
The pine trees breathe patient stillness
The pond beneath the willows fills itself
    with the poisoned sighs of melancholy

The pond's mirror flashes from afar
The poor man who died lonely in spirit steps waxen
    over an ancient path
The poppy bloomed silver also, and carried our nightly star-dreams
    in its green capsules
The pregnant body chills
The priest's bell peals through the brown village
The purple rearing of a candle's flame
The quiet nearby reflects on things
    forgotten, extinguished angels
The rain hissed all night long and refreshed the meadow
The ravens at midday with their harsh caw
The red evening sky's rosy luster lay on the frozen peak, and his heart
    rang softly in the twilight
The red evening wind rattles through the window
The red gold of my heart
The red maple rustles
The red poppy
The red wine sways on rusty trellises
The reed rustles
The river dawns in greens, silver the ancient avenues
    and the towers of the city
The roar of a train from the arched bridge
The roof of dried straw still arches
The round eyes mirror the dark gold of the spring afternoon
The roundelay of the living appears unreal
The sacred dusking of blue above the mutilated forest
    and a dark bell chimes long
    in the village, peaceful cortège
The sadness above your eyelids
The saint's flesh melts away on a glowing grate
The Savior's black head wreathed in thorns
The scent of bread wafts through fever's blackness

The scream of rats in the empty courtyard
The sexton has the key
The shacks of the villagers have shut themselves
    in silence, and the frightening blue lament
    of the mountain stream in a black lull
The shadow of a black horse sprang from the dark
    and startled him
The shadow of evil reared above his head
The shadows of glorious times
The shadows of priestly princes, noble women
The shadows of rot in bare branches
The shadows of the elm trees fell upon me
The shadows of the old under the open door, where Helian's soul
    sees itself in a rosy mirror
The shape of the dead woman peals softly in the blue evening
The shepherd calls his frightened flock
The shepherds' dark shapes by the old pond
The shepherd's mellow pipes died
The sick scream in the hospital
The sick sit silently in the sunshine
The sighs of lovers breathe in the branches
The silence of gray clouds, yellow hill of rocks
The silence of night is wonderful
The silence of rotten crosses on the hill
The silent face of night
The silent female monk
The silent god lowers blue lids upon him
The silent house and the legends of the forest
The silver voice of the wind in the hallway
The simple silence of golden forests
The sister appears in autumn and black decay
The sisters have gone to white old men far away
The sister's mouth whispers in black branches

The sister's shadow reels through the silent grove, to greet
    the ghosts of heroes, the bleeding heads
The sister's sleep is heavy
The sister's slender figure emerged from the blue
    mirror, and like a dead man he fell into darkness
The skipper's ominous calls
The sky celebrates in bare branches
The sky hardens to gray over yellow fields
The sky is lonely and vast
The sky smiles down silently
The sleeper still whispers
The small blind girl runs trembling through
    the avenue
The small child in the straw hut
The small inn along the way appears to the traveler
The snow sank softly beneath dark steps
The soft leaves that fall into silence
The solitude of cliffs is all around
The son enters his father's empty house
The son of Pan appears in the guise of an excavator
    who sleeps through noon by the smoldering asphalt
The soul is a stranger on earth
The soul sang death, the flesh's green decay
The soul too in angelic silence
The soul's peace
The soul's silence begets blue springtime
The sounding one is enfolded by the purple arms of his star
    that climbs to uninhabited windows
The specters of the slain sigh in the shade of the autumn ash
The spirit of evil appeared in the shade of the walnut tree
The spirit of evil watches from its silver mask
The spirit of the one who died young appeared silently in the room
The stable lamp shines upon the cattle's balmy sleep

The starry sky
The stars are spreading white melancholy
The steps of madness in black rooms
The stern chambers and the forefathers' old belongings
The strange sister appears again in someone's evil dreams
The stranger is buried
The student, perhaps a doppelgänger, watches long after her
    from the window
The sun breaks from a sinister gorge
The sun has sunk into black linen; again and again
    this bygone evening returns
The sun of ancient days shines over Sonja's white
    eyebrows, snow that moistens her cheeks
The sun shines through your hands
The sun wants to appear black
The sun-youth's moist locks float
The sweet coat of an unknown woman
The sweet temper of a bluish view grazes
    beneath greening ash trees: golden repose
The sweetness of incense on the purple night wind
The sweetness of our wretched childhood
The swoosh of a colorful ring-a-ring dance
The table is set for many guests
The traveler enters in silence
The unborn descendants
The valley at night breathes blue chill
The voices of the reed and of quarreling men behind him, the one
    in the red barge rocks over freezing autumn waters, living
    in the dark myths of his sex, his stony eyes opening
    across nights and virgin horrors
The voices of women who have long been dead weave
    gently and in dark colors
The walls stare bare and gray with dirt into cool darkness

The walnut's dream-shape looms ineffably
The watchman's cry rings through blue air
The waters shimmer in greens and blues
The water's solemn rush
The way home is fraught with the gentle gloom of grazing herds
The wayfarer gently lifts his heavy eyelids
The wellspring's blue laughter and the black chill
    of night, when a wild hunter, I roused a snowy beast
The wheat bows lower
The whore who with icy chills gives birth to a dead child
The whorehouse peals with laughter
The wild elder bushes there, a long gone November day
The wild lament of their shattered mouths
The wilderness of forgotten hunts sank across
    moon-glazed forest paths
The willow weeps, silence stares
The willows stand wrapped in white shrouds, in which moths
    whirl in mad circles
The wind plunges through black alleyways
The wind pounds the rattling panes
The wine has been pressed, the mild silence filled with quiet
    replies to dark questions
The winter storm's wild organ-pipes resemble
    the dark rage of the people
The women sway their hips in lianas and fiery
    flowers, when the sea sings
The wood streams through evening harsh and pale
The yellow tresses of girls flutter
Their blueness mirrors the slumber of lovers
Their fleeting skills moan
Their flight resembles a sonata, full of faded chords
    and masculine gloom; softly a golden cloud dissipates
Their flowers are already in bloom, the grave violets

Their laughter got caught on small leaves
Their lives are so tangled, full of dreary plagues
Their moist lips tremble and they wait in archways
Their rosy sighs fell silent
Their shadows streak past the doe
Their wasting disease shuts itself in like a ghost
Their waxen-round gaze ponders golden times
Then a glimmering rain begins to fall
Then a tree begins to lift and spin before you
Then a whiff of decay makes me tremble
Then on the table bread and wine begin
        to shine in pure brightness
Then the black horses leap on a foggy pasture
Then the farmer says: It is good
Then the rats come up softly
Then the tears' wild torrents come crashing down
Then you also see a wrecked ship along the cliffs
Then you feel: it is good! in painful exhaustion
There a deserted terrace basks in the sun
There are rooms abuzz with chords and sonatas
There are shadows embracing before a blinded mirror
There are young girls in a courtyard in little dresses
        full of heartbreaking poverty
There rises and falls the motion of the reed
There shadows on the hill seek the resounding gold
There through boundless space the golden woodland softly flows
There's a tavern here for the lonely things
They are beating the drums
They circle and descend sevenfold in number
They emerge from the twilight
They move like helpless marionettes before death
Things bright-green bloom and others rot

Things greening, blossoming branches stir
    the crystal forehead; glimmering, rocking boat
This age breathes darker tears
This founders in peace and silence
This is your doom
This most strange garden of twilight trees
This place is for the foul rut of black toads
This recalls tree and animal
This shocks the stranger's breast
Thorny wilderness girds the city
Three men come in darkly through the gate
    with scythes shattered in the field
Through gardened frames of leaves twirls
    the laughter of fine ladies
Through the room spray blazing sparks
Through the twilight village
Thus a sparse green moves the stranger's knee
Thus above clouds I follow their journeys
Thus the lamps went out in the cold chambers, and suffering people
    gazed mutely at each other from behind crimson masks
Time trickles away
To greet his darling wife, comes a blackamoor
    toward you brown and raw
To his right, there appeared the lamenting figure
    of a white angel, and the cripple's shadow
    grew larger in the dark
To the rhythm of ships that rock on the river
To the rhythm of the violin's echo
Today they strew flowers blue and red
    on their crypts, which light up shyly
Today they tread the brown grapes
Torn terraces

Towering mountains in the tempest of night
Transforms into crimson dreams the pain and trouble
    of the stony life, so the thorny sting will never leave
    off the decaying body
Tritons emerge from the flood
Truly!
Twilight full of rest and wine
Twin mirrors framed by shadows and by slimy stones
Two black horses leap across the meadow
Two moons begin to sparkle in the eyes of the old stone woman
Two sleepers stagger homeward, gray and vague
Two wolves share their blood in a stony embrace

U

Under stiff hands fruit and tools decayed
    before the terrified descendants
Under the starred canvas, the lonely man
    walks through the silent midnight
Under whitewashed arches, where the swallow flew in
    and out, we drank fiery wine
Up into the blue organs swell
Uproar

V

Very quietly the sunflower enjoys its gold and melts away
Very softly evening's blue wing stirs
Very softly her smile sinks into the crumbling well
    that murmurs bluish in the twilight
Violently a black horse rears up; the maid's hyacinthine
    locks strain at the heat of its purple nostrils

W

Wandering along the black walls
    of evening, silver the lyre of Orpheus
    sounds forth in the dark mere
Was it love?
Wasted hope of life
Watching the gray gulls
Wayfarer in the black wind; dry reeds whisper softly
We drink the white waters of the pond
What is entwined comes silvery undone
What lust!
What makes you stand still on rotten stairs
    in your forefathers' house: leaden blackness
What was it she called? Don't you know it?
Wheat rustles all around, cut by reapers in the afternoon
When a fat rat gnaws at door and chest
When an iron-willed angel approaches man in the grove
When animal fumes waft through the room
When autumn arrived, he walked, a clairvoyant, across
    brown meadows
When autumn has come
When depth grows immeasurably
When evening comes
When evening has arrived
When every destiny has been fulfilled in defiled rooms, death enters
    the house with putrid steps
When glowing with blossoms you rouse her
    sprouting life, its high past prompting
When he lay in his cold bed, he was
    suddenly overwhelmed by untold tears
When he stretches his arms and legs astonished

When he threw himself like a stone before raging black horses
When his blood is haunted by her stars
When I sleepwalked past rooms of stone, and a quiet little lamp
    stood burning in each one, a copper candelabrum, and when
    I sank shivering onto my bed, the black shadow
    of a female stranger stood again by my head, and silently
    I hid my face in my slow hands
When I took your slender hands, you opened
    your round eyes softly
When I walked in the twilight garden, and the black figure of evil
    had left me, I was enfolded by the hyacinthine silence of night
When in the evening
When in the evening we were gentle playmates
When man in his chamber dwelled on righteous
    thoughts, in mute prayers soared
    around God's living head
When night falls
When night fell, his heart broke like crystal, and darkness
    struck his brow
When Orpheus stirs the silvery lute, mourning
    something dead in the evening garden
When peaceful monks, we pressed the crimson grape
When that March the moon crumbled
When the angel's silvery voice died in Sebastian's shadow
When the boy softly descended to cool waters
    silver fish, the silence, and the face
When the day bows out in silence
When the servants beat the gentle eyes with nettles
When the snow falls against the window
When the soul dreams cooler blossoms
When they woke, the stars above their heads went out
When we behold a stone face in black waters
When we thirst

When you lay your forehead into silver hands
Where are the terrible paths of death?
Where are you, heavenly countenance?
Where are you, you who walked by my side?
Where cold and evil
Where earlier the holy brother walked
Where friends come together after their meal
Where in the shade of autumn elms
    the crumbling path falls away
Where perhaps the thrush still sings
Where purple grapes hang thick
Where quiet pilgrims are waiting
Where she stands in her slender dream-shape
Where solitude dwells and the maples rustle
Where suddenly the blue falls strangely silent
Where the cedar, a delicate creature, unfolds
    beneath the father's blue eyebrows
Where the poplar looms in silver shades, stars
    and stones are
Where the young novice crowns himself with brown leaves
Where the wild grass hisses brownish now
Where your moonlike eyes are
Wherever you go, you bring autumn and evening
While lanterns shatter in the storm by night
While like the pale children's death-dance
While the lids widen before godship
While the trees bloom in the night, to cover
    death's countenance
Whispers in the reeds and a floating back
White birds flutter up at night's edge
White girl beneath the wild oak, and the thorn
    bloomed silver
White high priest of truth

White sleep!
White voices straying through eerie courtyards
Who are you, calm thing beneath the tall trees?
Whose breath comes to caress me?
Why raise your silver hand to your eyes; and your eyelids sink
    as if drunk with poppy?
Wild birds' migrations
Wild fruit falls blackish from trees at night
Wild wolves broke through the gate
Windless calm of the soul
Windless, starless night
Window, brilliant beds of flowers
With a crimson forehead he entered the moor, and God's wrath
    whipped his metallic shoulders
With a darkened mind the idiot speaks a word
    of love that fades away in the black bush
With black wings night stirs the boy's temple
With blood and weapon-fray of forgotten times
    the water soughs in the pine ground
With bony hands unhallowed childhood gropes
    for fairy tales in the blue
With dark looks lovers gaze at each other
With deadly weapons, the golden plains
With evening dreams boys play
    scattershot there at the fountain
With figures of dead heroes, moon, you fill
    the silent forests
With flying tresses, and she receives with blessed silence
    the rutting suitor, and trembling with deep shivers
    of your wild, storm-raging embrace
With fractured eyebrows, silver arms
With lunar wings the sister's white face rose
    over greening treetops and crystal cliffs

With silver soles I descended the thorny steps, and I entered
    the lime-washed chamber
With steps of stone you tramp along the railway
    banks, with round eyes, like a soldier who storms
    a black entrenchment
Withered grave and even the year looks out from tree and beast
Woe, that I have forgotten it!
Woe, the scream of the woman giving birth
Woe, the stony eyes of the sister, when at supper her madness
    appeared on his nightly forehead, when the bread turned
    to stone beneath the mother's suffering hands
Woe to the stooped appearance of women
Woe to the unspeakable guilt this heart proclaims
Woe, you golden shivers of death
Women carry entrails in baskets
Women sing and toil in the fields
    into which cloister bells peal
Wonderfully an Eden sinks into the sand
Wonderfully lovers on a sweet journey
    drift by on the pond
World-misery ghosts through the afternoon
Worms drip from their yellowed eyelids
Wound, red, never shown in dark rooms
    enables life, where the blue bells ring

X

Y

Yellow fields stream into noon
Yellowed fruit smells sweeter
Yet always Pan's son sleeps in the gray marble
Yet from branches a gentle spirit beckons
Yet it seemed to him: here I lived my forgotten years
Yet sometimes the soul brightens, when it recalls
    happy men, dark-gold days of spring
You, a blue animal trembling in silence; you, the pale priest
    who slaughters it on the black altar
You—a crimson moon, as the other appears
    in the green shade of the olive tree
You, a green metal and inside a fiery face that wants to go forth
    and from atop the hill of bones sing of dark times
    and the angel's blazing fall
You also mourn, you gentle gods
You always think the white face of mankind
You appear, Elis, a resting man with round eyes
You are vast, dark mouth within, figure
    shaped by autumn clouds
You buffoon!
You can barely hear the crickets' song
You come as in a dream
You dream: the sister combs her blonde hair
You dying races!
You emerge white in the friend's autumnal landscape
You evening bells long and soft
    in parting lend good spirits
You feel your heart mad with bliss
You fool!
You gray flowers overflowing with hellish grimaces

You great cities
You I love truly, my rough washerwoman
You laugh out loud, brown Gret crazed the sea
    dreams in the mind, while a just-withered rose
    blows down before me
You live silently in the shadow
    of the autumn ash tree, sunken in the hill's
    righteous measure
You moon-devoured shadows sighing
    in the empty crystal of the mountain lake
You mountains cool and blue!
You on the rotten stairs: tree, star, stone!
You see her standing spellbound
You sense commotion in the sky
You soldiers!
You step among your womankind
You still hear the teacher's lingering fiddle
You, still wild, who conjures rosy islands
    from brown tobacco clouds, and from within
    fetches the savage cry of a griffin hunting around
    black cliffs in sea, storm, and ice
You streams, dusking far into the distance!
You wild mountains, the eagle's noble sorrow
Your blue coat enfolded the one sinking
Your body is a hyacinth
    into which a monk
    dips the waxen fingers
Your crystal face
Your dress rustles on the winding stairs
Your eyelids are heavy with poppy and dream
    silently upon my brow
Your face

Your legs rattle in stride like blue ice and a smile
     full of sorrow, and pride has petrified your face
     and your forehead pales before the lust of frost
Your lips drink the coolness of the blue rock-spring
Your lost shadow in the sunset glow
Your red mouth sealed the friend's aberration
Your stars close into evil signs
Your wild fissures I sing
Youth, from your crystal mouth
     your golden gaze sank to the valley

Z

ABOUT THE TRANSLATOR AND AUTHORS

Daniele Pantano is a Swiss poet, translator, critic, and editor. His individual poems, essays, and reviews, as well as his translations from the German by Friedrich Dürrenmatt, Georg Trakl, and Robert Walser, have appeared in numerous magazines, journals, and anthologies worldwide. Pantano's poetry has been translated into several languages, including German, Albanian, Bulgarian, Kurdish, and Farsi. Pantano taught at the University of South Florida, served as the Visiting Poet-in-Residence at Florida Southern College, and directed the Creative Writing program at Edge Hill University, England, where he was Reader in Poetry and Literary Translation. Pantano lives somewhere at the end of a line. For more information, please visit www.pantano.ch.

Georg Trakl (1887–1914) is commonly seen as one of the leading figures of the Austro-German expressionist movement in literature during the early part of the twentieth century.